Mar 2015

Surprising Experiments with
Sound

Text: Paula Navarro & Àngels Jiménez
Illustrations: Bernadette Cuxart

BARRON'S

Contents

Objectives of this book

This book *Surprising Experiments with Sound* is the first of 4 books in the "Magic Science" series and provides children aged 6 to 12 with a series of experiments related to everyday phenomena in their lives, such as sound.

The 16 experiments presented in this book include handicraft works that can be done at home or at school, with an educational background.

The book explains in an educational manner what sound is, how it is made, how the voice box works, what resonance and sound amplification mean, how sound is conveyed through different means, how sound is reproduced using an instrument, and finally, how sound behaves in the different objects surrounding us.

By conducting these experiments, the children will enjoy two things for having fun and awakening curiosity (the handicraft work and the science that lies behind every little thing): *Surprising Experiments with Sound* encourages dexterity with the hands and sharpens the hearing!

Jumping drum

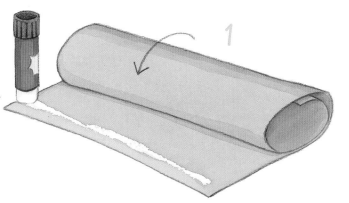

You will need:
- Construction paper
- Stick of glue
- Colored tape
- Two balloons
- Scissors
- A little rice

1 Cut construction paper to the size you want to make the sound tube. Then roll it up, trying to make a perfect circle (about the size of a kitchen towel roll) and secure it with glue.

2 Decorate the tube with colored tape, which will also help it to stick—a clever trick!

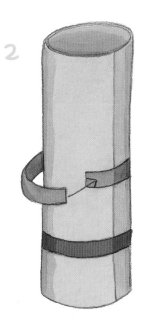

3 Strengthen both ends of the tube with more tape; you could even apply several layers. Stick the tape so that the tube is as strong inside as outside. If you like, you can decorate it with different tapes.

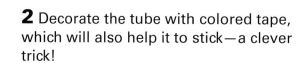

4 Take a balloon and cut it in half, to make a beheaded balloon! In the next step, we will only use the widest part. Do the same with the other balloon.

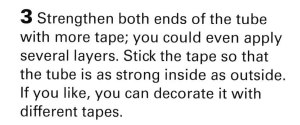

5 Place one of the balloons over one of the holes in the tube, making a membrane covering the hole. Place the other balloon on the other end, covering both holes well. It is better to ask for help for this part, because it's quite hard to stop them jumping off!

Why does it happen?

Sound is movement; it is a longitudinal wave. And what does that mean? The vibration produced is always conveyed forward. When you tap the bottom membrane, the sound is transmitted through the air, as if the air particles were dominoes standing in a row and you make them fall one on the other. Each particle touches the one next to it and transmits the vibration received.

The air impact reaches the upper membrane and, by causing it to vibrate, the rice also vibrates and is made to jump.

6 Try it out!
Place a little rice on one of the membranes. Warm your hand and tap the bottom membrane. Don't get carried away tapping, otherwise you won't see the jumping rice effect.

Traveling sound

You will need:
- ◆ Three small bottles or similar containers
- ◆ Water
- ◆ Flour or sugar
- ◆ Lentils or rice
- ◆ A spoon
- ◆ A funnel (optional)

1 Take the empty bottle and the spoon. First place the bottle near your ear, as if you were making a sandwich between your head and the spoon! Tap the bottle with the spoon to see what happens and what you hear.

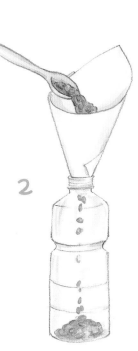

2 Now fill this bottle to the top with dried lentils.

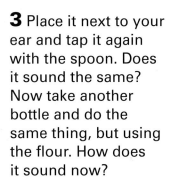

3 Place it next to your ear and tap it again with the spoon. Does it sound the same? Now take another bottle and do the same thing, but using the flour. How does it sound now?

4 Fill a third and final bottle with water. Don't drink it yet! Use a funnel to fill it and avoid spilling it on the table. Place the bottle next to your ear and tap it again. Does it sound like the others?

5 Tap the three bottles containing lentils, flour, and water one after the other and compare the sound to find out what tone each substance gives. If you want to go a step further, place a bottle next to each ear and gets somebody else to tap them: It sounds like a song!

6 Try it out!

Try to fill more bottles with different things you have at home, at school, or in the park: soap, sand, screws… The interesting thing about this experiment is discovering that the bottles sound different depending on what you put inside them. You'll be surprised.

Why does it happen?

They sound different because sound is not transmitted in the same way through all mediums. It passes through water much faster than through air, and if there were no air we wouldn't even be able to hear it, as happens in space. So, **sound needs a medium,** a vehicle, **in order to be transmitted,** and depending on its qualities you can hear stronger or weaker. Dolphins and whales communicate over long distances through water, over dozens of miles! Imagine that a friend could hear you over such a great distance!

Alien ears

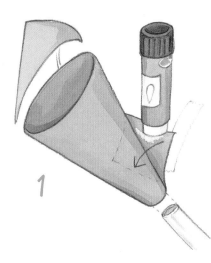

1 Take a sheet of construction paper and cut it to make a cone. Make sure that the plastic tube can pass through the hole in the small end. Stick the edges with glue and tape. Then make another cone the same shape.

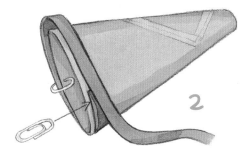

You will need:
- ◆ Tape
- ◆ Glue
- ◆ Plastic tube or hose
- ◆ Thick elastic thread
- ◆ Paper clips
- ◆ Colored construction paper

2 Wrap the elastic around the cone and secure it in place with 2 paper clips. Then place it over your ear and pass the elastic over your head to measure where you should position the other cone. Keep track of the distance and wrap the other end around the other cone. Also fasten it with 2 paper clips.

3 Take the hanging end of the elastic and take it to the other ear as if it were a headband, to keep it in place better. You can secure it with the other paper clip on the other part so that it is more secure.

4 Cut the plastic tube the same length as your arm. Pass it through the small opening of the cone and secure it with tape. It should not move or pinch.

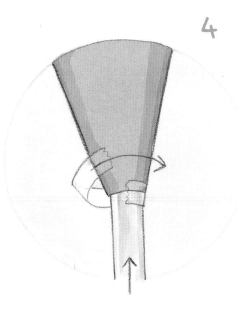

5 Make 2 larger cones and do the same thing, but attach them onto the other ends of the tubes. See if you can remember how!

5

6 Try it out!
Take the large cones in your hands, close or blindfold your eyes, and try to discover where the sounds are coming from! Try crossing over the tubes. Sound coming from the right will be heard in the left ear, and vice versa! How confusing!

6

Why does it happen?

Our ears are separated, and that's why the sound we hear in one is different from what we hear in the other. It serves to better locate the **point of origin of the sound.** To determine this, our brain compares what it hears on each side, so we hear in stereo! Some animals can move their ears to better locate their prey or predator. Antelopes, impalas, and zebras move their ears to make sure the lion doesn't take them by surprise and eat them!

An improvised umpire

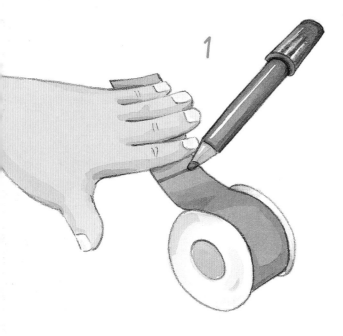

1 Measure and cut out a piece of cellophane about four fingers wide. If you have small fingers, make it wider!

You will need:
◆ Scissors
◆ Cellophane tape
◆ Permanent markers

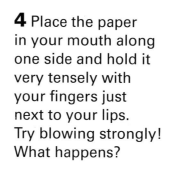

2 Cut out the piece of paper you have measured. You must cut it very straight! Also, cut off the four corners so that they are rounded and the paper makes a noise better.

3 Decorate the piece of paper on the front and back to make it prettier! Draw with the marker pen, making it permanent.

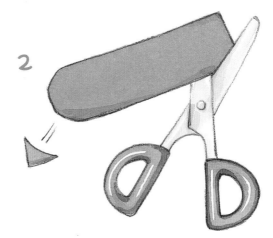

4 Place the paper in your mouth along one side and hold it very tensely with your fingers just next to your lips. Try blowing strongly! What happens?

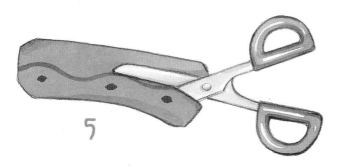

5 Now you can cut the tape in half. Try your funny whistle again!

6 Try it out!
You will observe that different sounds are made according to the width of the tape.

Why does it happen?
When you place the tape very close to your lips and blow very hard, you make the tape vibrate; **it moves very fast.** That's how an intense whistle is made, which sounds like an umpire's whistle! Now you know what to do if you ever play a game and somebody forgets the umpire's whistle!

A homemade sax

1 Cut the bottle in half. It's best to stick the scissors in first and then cut it. If the plastic is too hard, ask an adult to help you.

You will need:
- Construction paper
- A small water bottle
- A balloon
- Scissors
- A straw
- Rubber bands

2 You're left with the neck of the bottle (you won't need the other part for the experiment). Make a hole under the cut large enough to pass a straw through. You could also use a hole punch if it's too hard with the scissors.

3 Roll the construction paper into a thin tube and place it inside the neck of the bottle. Then secure it in the middle with a rubber band so the tube does not open up. Once the tube is inside the bottle, you can remove the rubber band. Then the construction paper will open up slightly and fit inside tightly. You can use the rubber band to secure the construction paper in the neck of the bottle.

4 Cut the balloon a bit higher than halfway and keep the widest part. Place it over the opening in the bottle, forming a membrane and closing the opening. The construction paper tube should be positioned so that it touches the membrane.

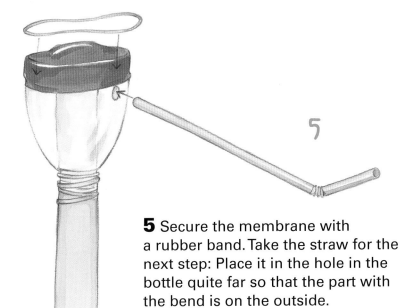

5 Secure the membrane with a rubber band. Take the straw for the next step: Place it in the hole in the bottle quite far so that the part with the bend is on the outside.

Why does it happen?

When you blow through the straw, you introduce air into the bottle in the area between the membrane and the construction paper tube. The pressure of the air trying to escape through the tube makes the membrane move, which is elastic and thus **vibrates**. If you touch the membrane with your finger, you will feel it vibrate. These **vibrations** are the sound you hear!

6 Try it out!
Fill your lungs with air and blow through the straw! Toot! You have a homemade saxophone!

13

The singer scares the salt!

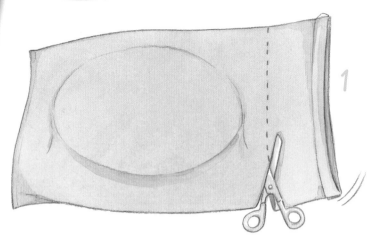

1 Place the (empty and clean!) trash bag over the glass dish. Cover it well and measure where you need to cut it. Don't open it; cut it as it is, with two layers of plastic.

2 Place two rubber bands around the bag to secure it. Then stretch the bag at the bottom so that the surface is very tense.

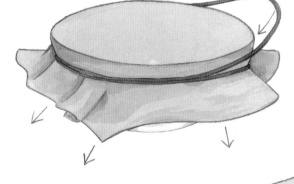

3 When the bag is as smooth as a drum, cut off the overlapping edges. Cut carefully, leaving a straight well-cut edge.

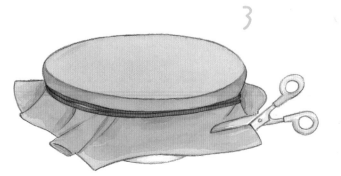

4 Prepare the salt to place on the bag. You could make colored salt by rubbing colored chalk on it.

5 Take a large spoon, fill it with the salt and cover the surface of the bag. Spread the salt all over the bag with the spoon, without spilling it!

Why does it happen?

When you shout, your voice reaches the bag and makes it **vibrate.** The vibration is transmitted to the salt and causes it to move! If you change your tone of voice, you change the oscillation and the salt moves differently. The dish acts as a **voice box** and strengthens the effect. We have an extraordinary device, which is our voice tract. The respiratory apparatus together with the vocal chords and the mouth form an instrument capable of modulating sharp and deep tones, just like a flute or a guitar.

6 Try it out!

Approach the dish, but stay a palm's distance away. Fill your lungs with air and shout loudly! It is the SALT SONG!!! It's important to sustain the note, that is, to lengthen the same note. You will see that the patch of salt jumps and changes shape. You can try different sounds, sharp and deep!

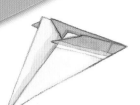

A paper bomb

You will need:
- Two different colored sheets of paper
- Ruler
- Scissors
- Tape
- Stickers for decoration (optional)

1 Take the colored paper you like the best! If you're not sure, toss a coin! Fold the paper in half, take one of the corners and fold it again making a triangle on one layer of paper.

2 Make this fold in order to cut out the square, first marking with a pencil the line along which you have to cut. Don't make a mistake; it's a delicate step! Then cut the other side and you have a square! Magic? No, paper and scissor skills!

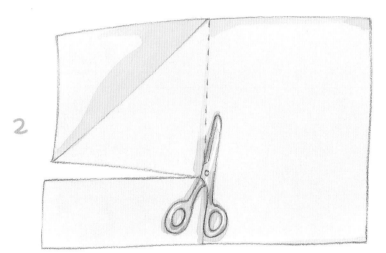

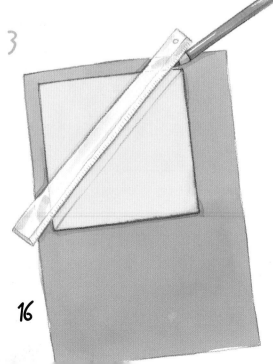

3 Place the square on top of the other sheet of paper, leaving a couple of fingers' distance along the sides. Place the ruler 1 cm from each side diagonally and draw a line without drawing on the frame. When you have made the mark, remove the square and finish drawing the line along which you must cut the triangle and cut it.

4 Carefully place the square on top of the triangle and fold in the overlapping parts. Secure it with a little tape.

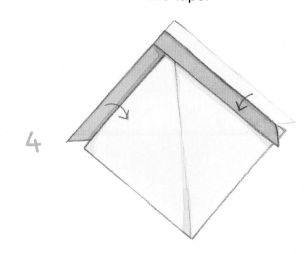

5 Turn the paper upside down and fold the square diagonally along the line so that the triangle is in the inside. It looks like a paper airplane, so why let's not fly it?

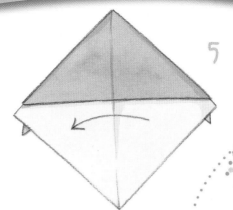

6 Try it out!

Hold the paper at the bottom, raise your arm above your head, and throw it down sharply and as fast as possible. BOOM! The paper unfolds and makes a sound like a firework!

Why does it happen?

When you lower your arm, the air enters the paper suddenly, forming a **shock wave,** which is the "boom" that we hear. Shock waves occur when you move faster than the speed of sound and are characterized by a sudden loud and surprising sound. The same thing happens when a firework goes off or you shake a can strongly.

Listen to the megaphone!

1 Wash the inside of the bottle well. Remove the lid and ring and place them in the plastics recycling bin! You may have to ask an adult for help if it's hard to remove the ring.

2 Mark the cutting line on the bottle with a pen, so it is easier to cut in a straight line. Of course, you need to have a steady hand to avoid a wavy line!

3 Take the scissors (ideally large and strong, because it's hard) and pierce the tip through the bottle just above the line you've drawn. If the plastic is very hard, you'll have to ask for a hand again!

4 Strengthen the cut in the middle of the container with a little colored tape to make it prettier and also to make the opening smoother. Stick some tape on the upper part around the hole and leave a margin in order to stick it inside the container.

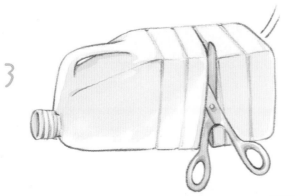

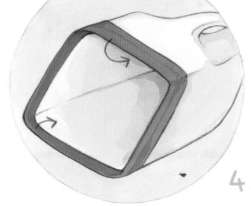

5 Decorate the container with things you like and can find at home—streamers, tape, and stickers—to make it very pretty!

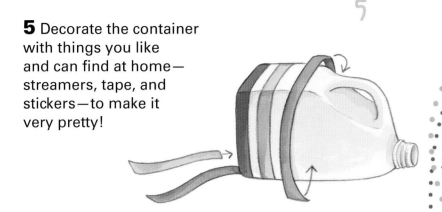

6 Try it out!

Now you have a very original super megaphone! Almost like the one used by the police and protestors, but much more colorful! For everybody to hear you, you simply have to place the megaphone in front of your mouth, cover the edges of your lips so that it sounds louder, and shout: Listen up! Listen up! We have a megaphone!

Why does it happen?

The conical shape of the container (smaller at the mouth than the opening) **amplifies** the sound of our voice. So, when you speak through the megaphone, your voice is heard louder than when you speak normally. That's why many wind instruments end in a conical shape. Thus the sound is heard louder without being next to it. Now that you have an amplifier, are you ready to lead your own protests? Listen up! Listen up!

Spoon bell

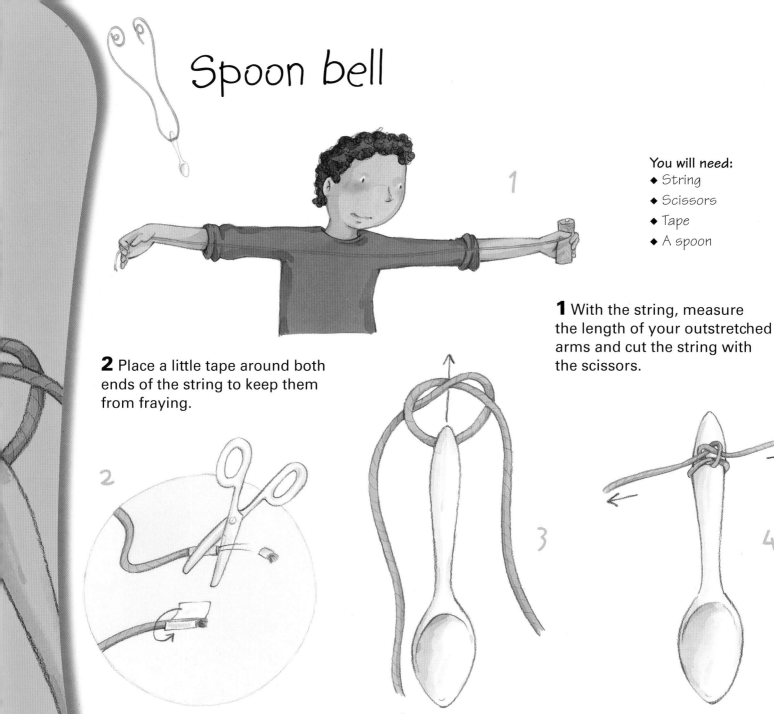

You will need:
- ◆ String
- ◆ Scissors
- ◆ Tape
- ◆ A spoon

1 With the string, measure the length of your outstretched arms and cut the string with the scissors.

2 Place a little tape around both ends of the string to keep them from fraying.

3 Tie a knot in the middle of the string without pulling. Pass the spoon through the hole, and now pull the knot very tightly.

4 Now tie another knot in the spoon so that it cannot slide out.

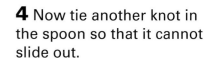

5 Wrap the ends of the string around your fingers and place them next to your ears (at the eardrum, but on the outside). You don't need to place them inside your ears, especially if your hands are dirty! Hold the string with your fingers.

Why does it happen?

The spoon bangs against the table or the wall and the impact causes it to vibrate. The vibration is transmitted along the string almost without losing intensity, which is why when it reaches our ears, we hear it very loudly. It's as if our ears were next to the spoon. **Some materials promote the transmission of sound and others do the opposite.** Metals convey sound very well, which is why many musical instruments are made of these materials. Have you ever seen anybody play a cotton instrument?

6 Try it out!
Swing the spoon (like a pendulum) and make it bang against the table or the wall. You will notice that it sounds like a real church bell: DING-DONG! Or like the bells cows wear around their necks.

Gulp, gulp... Hello?

You will need:
- Two plastic or paper cups
- Scissors
- Tape
- String
- Permanent markers
- Pen
- Stickers

1 Decorate the cups to make them fun and bright. You can make drawings with markers or put stickers on them—or both!

2 Then turn the cups upside down on the table. Make a small hole in the bottom of the cup (ouch!) with the scissors and enlarge them to the required size with the tip of a pen.

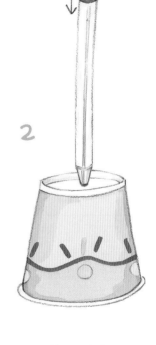

3 The connecting string must be at least twice the length of your outstretched arms. To communicate between one end of the house and the other, you will need much longer string, but be careful, as it might get caught in the furniture!

4 Place a little tape on both ends of the string to keep them from fraying. Then pass one end of the string through the hole in one of the cups, from outside inward.

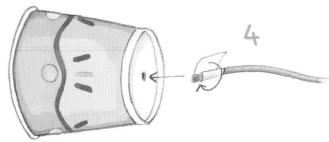

5 Pull the string and tie a double knot. Make sure it's not a slipknot and pull the string from outside the cup so that the knot touches the bottom of the cup and does not escape. Test it well: Is the knot still there? Do the same with the other end of the string and the other cup.

Why does it happen?

When you speak into the cup, your voice is transmitted along the string. As you've seen before, the **tension** helps the transmission of sound. Try speaking with the string tense and slack. Do you notice the difference? The cup also acts as a sound **amplifier,** so when you place it over your ear you can hear the other person perfectly.

6 Try it out!

Choose somebody to have a conversation with through the cups: Mom, Dad, a brother or sister, the neighbor on the fifth floor, or whomever you like. Each person takes a cup, one places it over the mouth, and the other places it over the ear to listen. Pull the string tightly so that the sound can be conveyed well and... Now you can speak over the phone! No matter how far apart you go, you will hear the other person as if they were beside you!

Play the straw!

1 Take a straw and flatten the tip using your teeth (if it's a bendy straw, flatten the end you don't drink from). It will look like you're frowning.

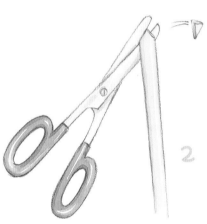

2 Cut the flattened end in the shape of a triangle. First make a diagonal cut on one side and then the other. Be careful with your fingers!

3 Wet your lips, circling your tongue around them several times. You could imagine you're eating a delicious chocolate ice cream! Mmm... This step enables the lips to vibrate. Try vibrating a sound without the straw!

4 Inhale, place the straw in your lips, and blow through it very hard—without making a face as red as a tomato! If you've done well, the straw will make a sound almost as lovely as a flute.

5 Now cut the straw as you blow. If it's too complicated, ask somebody to cut the straw while you blow. The sound changes as you cut. Can you notice? The straw vibrates as you blow. If you place your fingers gently on it, you will feel the vibration.

Why *does* it happen?

When you place the cut straw in your mouth and blow closing your lips, you make the straw vibrate. When you put your finger on the straw, you feel the vibrations, the sound you hear!

As you cut the straw, the sound becomes sharper, because the smaller straw vibrates faster that the longer straw. The **shorter** the straw, the **sharper** the sound; the **longer** the straw, the **deeper** the sound. This also occurs with musical instruments.

6 **Try it out!**

In order to hold a concert, you will need to make different musical notes so you can play the straw with your family and friends. Cut seven straws in different lengths. You will find that the longest straw is the deepest and the shortest is the sharpest.

Musical box

1 Let's decorate the box! Some wrapping paper you have at home would be ideal. Place the box in the middle of the paper, mark the base, and enlarge the lines along the sides an inch longer than the height of the sides.

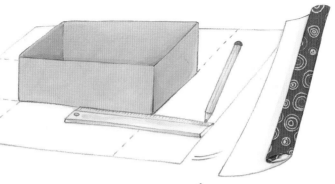

You will need:
- A cardboard box (e.g., shoebox)
- Rubber bands
- Scissors
- Colored wrapping paper (optional)
- Glue

2 Look at the picture to draw the four flaps you will use to join the sides together. Cut along the lines and remove the excess paper.

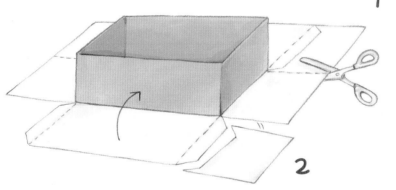

3 Apply some glue and cover the sides, smoothing them with your hands to prevent wrinkles.

4 Don't forget the inside—you must also decorate it the same! Cover all the insides and the end result looks nothing like at the start. It's so pretty!

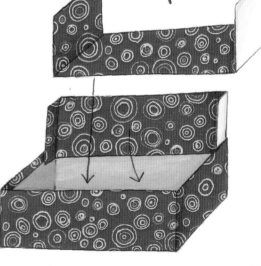

5 Take some rubber bands and place them around the box, separated and well distributed along the box. Imagine a musical instrument such as a harp or a violin, and that will help you to position the rubber bands similarly! You can ask an adult to help you to keep them from breaking and pinging off.

Why does it happen?

When we strike the rubber bands and pluck them with our fingers, we make them vibrate, and vibration is the key to the sound! The vibration is amplified inside the box we have decorated, which acts as a **soundboard,** exactly like a guitar. This echo is amplified, reaches our ears, and we can hear the music.

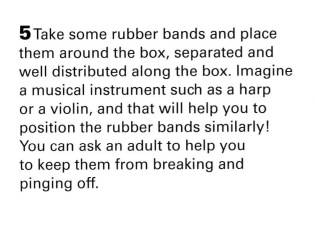

6 Try it out!

Now you can start playing your musical instrument! Pluck them like the strings of a guitar and you will hear that the rubber bands make amazing sounds. Can you play a solo?

Shhh... Breathe in and count to 3

You will need:
- 2 small plastic bottles
- Scissors
- Rubber bands
- 3 balloons
- A transparent piece of plastic tube or hose

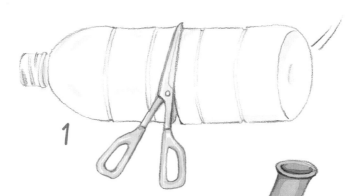

1 Stick the scissors in one of the bottles about halfway and cut it as straight as possible. To do so well, it's best to turn the bottle from the bottom. First cut one and then the other.

2 Take one of the balloons and cut off the narrow part or the neck of the balloon. Place it over the neck of the cut bottle. Do the same with the other bottle—but with a different balloon, of course!

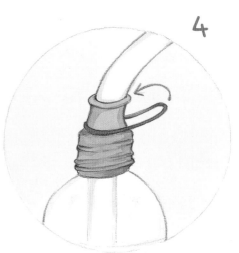

3 Pass the plastic tube through one of the balloons beyond the neck of the bottle.

4 Secure the tube and the balloon with a rubber band so that the hole is well sealed. Wrap the rubber band around it several times so that the tube stays in. Do the same with the other bottle: Pass the tube through the balloon and secure it tightly with a rubber band!

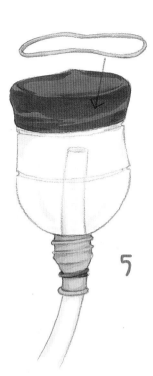

5 Cut the third balloon in the same way, but this time you need the bottom part (you can use one of the parts left over from the other balloons). Cover the wide part of the bottle with the balloon, forming a membrane (like a drum). Wrap a rubber band around it to secure it.

Why **does** it happen?

The heart beats cause the membrane at the end of your stethoscope to vibrate, and this is transmitted to your ear, **focusing** it, so that you can clearly hear your heartbeat or that of somebody else.

6 Try it out!

Place the bottle with the membrane at the heart, so that if you listen very carefully in a quiet place, you will be able to hear... THE BEAT OF YOUR HEART! Yes, like when the doctor listens to you! Try to listen to somebody else's heartbeat!

Bottle orchestra

You will need:
- 7 empty one-liter glass bottles
- Jug of water
- Teaspoon
- Permanent marker

1 You need 7 one-liter glass bottles, preferably all the same. So, whenever a bottle is emptied at home, collect it! When you have them all, fill one of them all the way; it will make the deepest note.

2 Fill the other bottles with less water each time, to obtain the musical notes (Do, Re, Mi, Fa, So, La and Ti). Fill each one so that it has about 2 fingers' width of water less than the previous. The emptiest one will have the highest note.

3 Get your ears ready. Clean the wax you may have in them, and then you can try tuning the bottles, adjusting the level slightly if you think the note is out of tune. To make it easier, compare the notes with a musical instrument.

4 When you have the notes, mark the particular musical scale on the bottle with a permanent marker, so that if anybody moves them you won't confuse the order.

30

5

5 Take a spoon and tap the bottles with it, always at the same level, trying to play a song you know.

Why *does* it happen?

The vibration is produced when the spoon hits the bottle and is transmitted through it and the water inside, making the bottles sound differently, as they are not all filled the same. So, when you tap them, you make the notes sound intentionally and in **harmony**, that is, in an order that is pleasing to our ears, making a lovely **tune**. And if it doesn't turn out well, you might end up with a headache!

6

6 Try it out!
Now you simply have to dare to compose your own songs. Maybe if it turns out well, you'll release a song next summer! Otherwise, try playing this song, HAPPY BIRTHDAY:

DO DO RE DO FA MI
DO DO RE DO SO FA
DO DO LA SO FA MI RE
LA LA SO FA SO FA

31

Rain stick!

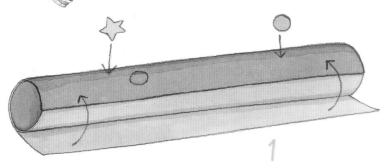

1 Decorate the tube nicely! Cover it with colored paper, securing it with a little bit of tape. You can also use different colored paper, making a collage, or you can add stickers!

You will need:
- A cardboard tube
- Tape
- Scissors
- Sheet of construction paper
- Clear adhesive covering
- Rice
- Colored paper
- Rubber bands
- Pencil

2 You must seal the ends of the tube. How? Cut out two circles of construction paper, the same size as the tube ends. It's best to place the tube on the construction paper, draw around it with a pencil, and then cut it out. Make two!

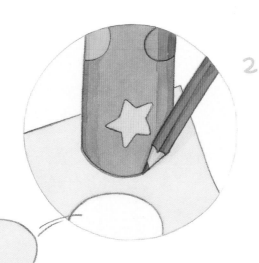

3 Place one of the circles on the transparent cover and draw a circle two fingers' width larger than the circle. Cut it out and do the same for the other one. Remove the paper and place the circles in the middle, sticky side up, otherwise you'll stick it to the table!

4 Stick one of the cover circles on one end of the tube to cover the hole. The cover must be stuck around the tube well. So that it holds better, secure it with a rubber band.

5 Turn the tube over and pour some rice in the other end, very carefully! Fill the tube a quarter of the way (half of halfway!). If you don't fill it enough, the rain won't last very long; and the same will happen if you fill it too much! Then cover the other end as before.

Why does it happen?

When heard together, the sound made by each grain of sand as it rolls down the tube is called white noise. **White noise** is the sum of many small sounds of different frequencies. Each grain of rice makes a different sound and when you hear them together a characteristic sound is made. You hear white noise when the rain falls on the leaves or on the ground, at the beach when the waves hit the sand or when the ventilator moves air molecules, etc.

6 Try it out!

Stretch out your arms, tilting the tube downwards, making the rice fall to the other end. What happens? It's started raining! Do the same thing turning it upside down. If you do so at different speeds, you will obtain different intensities of rainfall!

There's a rooster in my cup!

1 Take the cup and the paper clip. Open the clip to make a point and use it to make a hole in the bottom of the cup. Turn the paper clip to enlarge the hole, as you will have to pass the ribbon through it.

2 Choose a gift-wrapping ribbon. If it's very long, cut it shorter and thread it through the hole in the cup. It's best to fold it, otherwise it will be too thick to go through the hole. Then remove the end through the inside of the cup.

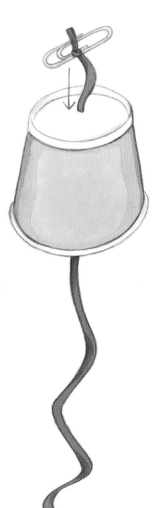

4 Take the cup and hold it firmly in your hand, allowing the ribbon to hang freely in the air. This type of ribbon is soft and flexible and will surely make a swirling shape.

3 Tie a paper clip onto the end of the ribbon outside the cup (not the same paper clip as before!). It's best to tie a few knots to secure it well.

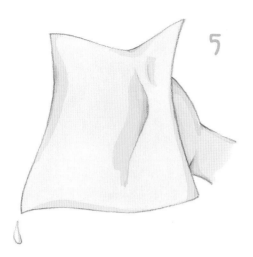

5 Moisten a cloth slightly and squeeze it so that it is not saturated. It only needs to be slightly damp. Hold it in the middle, as if you were holding a kitchen cloth to carefully pick up something hot.

Why *does* it happen?

As you slide the cloth down quickly, it transmits vibrations along the ribbon. The vibrations reach the cup that works like a **soundboard**, which is why the sound is so loud! The deepest sounding instruments, such as the double bass and cello, need much larger soundboards than those with sharp sounds. Have you ever noticed the size difference between a violin and a double bass?

6 Try it out!
With your free hand, hold the cloth around the top of the ribbon, squeezing slightly. Move it up and down several times. Listen to the noise it makes! If you do it well, it sounds like a rooster crowing!

Surprising Experiments with
Sound

First edition for the United States and Canada published in 2014 by Barron's Educational Series, Inc.

Copyright © Gemser Publications, S.L. 2014
C/ Castell, 38; Teià (08329) Barcelona, Spain (World Rights)
Tel: 93 540 13 53
E-mail: info@mercedesros.com
Website: mercedesros.com

Text: Paula Navarro & Àngels Jiménez

Illustrations: Bernadette Cuxart

Design and layout: Estudi Guasch, S.L.

All inquiries should be addressed to:
Barron's Educational Series, Inc.
250 Wireless Boulevard
Hauppauge, New York 11788
www.barronseduc.com

ISBN: 978-1-4380-0425-9

Library of Congress Control
   Number: 2013943423

Date of Manufacture: May 2014
Place of Manufacture: L. REX PRINTING COMPANY
   LIMITED, Dongguan City, Guangdong, China

Printed in China
9 8 7 6 5 4 3 2 1